THE HOW AND WHY WONDER® BOOK OF
SCIENCE EXPERIMENTS

Written by MARTIN L. KEEN
Illustrated by GEORGE J. ZAFFO
Editorial Production: DONALD D. WOLF

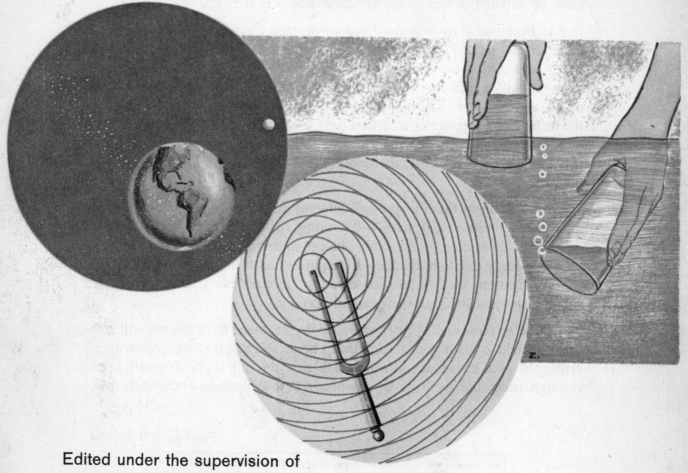

Edited under the supervision of
Dr. Paul E. Blackwood
Washington, D. C.

Text and illustrations approved by
Oakes A. White, Brooklyn Children's Museum, Brooklyn, New York

PRICE/STERN/SLOAN
Publishers, Inc., Los Angeles
1985

Introduction

The experiment is one of the scientist's ways of discovering new knowledge about the relationships of events in nature. Through experimenting, scientists can check on their speculations, their hunches, their guesses and their guiding ideas about what causes things to happen the way they do.

The How and Why Wonder®Book of Science Experiments provides suggested investigations in three very important areas of exploration — air and water, sound, and astronomy. By making these investigations, each young explorer will be rediscovering some of the principles of science. But in some of the activities, new knowledge will be discovered. For example, counting the meteors that appear at a certain time in a part of the sky will supply new facts — facts not known to anyone else. This is a real discovery. If reported properly, the facts may help astronomers refine the present knowledge about meteors.

This book shows that the study of different things in the world may require different techniques and tools — vibrating strings to study sound waves, scales and thermometers to study the air and water, telescopes and field glasses to study the stars. But they all require some of the same habits of careful investigation, such as keen observation, good thinking, accurate record keeping and painstaking experimentation.

Thus, *The How and Why Wonder®Book of Science Experiments* will be a helpful guide to assist young scientists at home and at school to explore interesting phases of knowledge. It will help them to develop skills of investigation through using the methods of discovery that experienced scientists use.

Paul E. Blackwood

Dr. Blackwood is a professional employee in the U. S. Office of Education. This book was edited by him in his private capacity and no official support or endorsement by the Office of Education is intended or should be inferred.

Contents

WATER VAPOR

RAIN

OXYGEN FROM AIR

CARBON DIOXIDE EXHALED BY MAN AND ANIMALS

Air and Water

Air and water are two materials with which everyone is familiar. We live at the bottom of an ocean of air, called the atmosphere. Air surrounds our bodies every minute of our lives, except when we are swimming or bathing. Air may be found in almost every open hollow in all materials on the surface of the earth. There is air also in many of the hollows and openings of the human body — for example, our ears, mouth, nose, and lungs. All animals breath air, and if deprived of it, they die.

The waters of seas, lakes, rivers, and streams cover three-quarters of the earth's surface. Water is necessary for life. The cells of which all living things are made are largely water. Water, given enough time, will dissolve almost any substance. This is important, be-

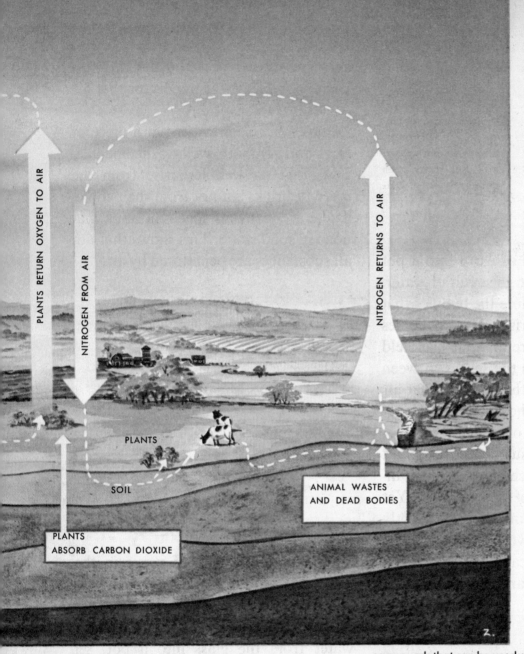

PLANTS RETURN OXYGEN TO AIR

NITROGEN FROM AIR

NITROGEN RETURNS TO AIR

PLANTS

SOIL

ANIMAL WASTES
AND DEAD BODIES

PLANTS
ABSORB CARBON DIOXIDE

ONE-CELLED ALGAE

The two major gases, nitrogen and oxygen, continually leave and then return to the atmosphere in endless processes, or cycles. Nitrogen from the air that penetrates the upper layers of the soil is changed by certain bacteria to chemical compounds that can be used as nourishment by plants. The plants may be eaten by animals that excrete compounds of nitrogen, which are decomposed by other bacteria, releasing nitrogen to the air. Dead plants and animals, too, are decomposed by bacteria in a process that eventually releases nitrogen to the air. The released nitrogen now may re-enter the soil — as the nitrogen cycle continues, over and over again. Oxygen is breathed by animals that exhale carbon dioxide. Plants absorb carbon dioxide from the air and give off oxygen that is again breathed by animals — as the oxygen cycle continues endlessly. Water falls from clouds as rain or snow. The fallen water forms streams and rivers that run into lakes and oceans. The heat of the sun evaporates water from these natural bodies of water. The evaporated water rises into the air as water vapor that cools to form clouds that produce more rain.

cause the materials that nourish living things are dissolved in water. This water makes up the main part of the blood of animals and the sap of plants, the two fluids that carry nourishing materials to the cells of living things.

We shall perform experiments concerning both air and water, because, as we shall see, these two materials are closely connected in many ways.

The bubbles are air that was held in the spaces between the particles of earth and freed when the earth was submerged in water.

How can you show that some materials hold air? Gently drop a clod of earth into a pot or glass full of water. Note the bubbles that arise. These bubbles are air that was held in the spaces between the particles of earth. The fact that air can penetrate into the soil is very important to the growth of plants. Probably the most needed substance for plant nourishment is the chemical element nitrogen. Four-fifths of air is nitrogen. Yet plants cannot obtain nitrogen directly from the air. However, certain bacteria that live in the soil can remove nitrogen from the air and change the nitrogen to

a form that can be used by plants. Thus, you can see why it is important that air penetrates soil.

Into some clean water put a piece of brick and a smooth, well-washed pebble. Note that air bubbles arise from the piece of brick, but not from the pebble. There are many air spaces in brick, but none in solid stone. This shows that not all substances are penetrated by air.

BRICK

PEBBLE

Air is trapped only in the brick, not the pebble.

The bubbles on the inside of the glass of water in the sun are air bubbles.

If you boil the water, more air boils out.

Place a clean glass of water in the sun. Look at it about an hour later. Do you see the bubbles on the inside of the glass? They are air bubbles. Pour the water from the glass into a pot, set the pot on a stove, and heat — but don't boil,— the water. Heating makes more air bubbles arise from the water and some form around the sides of the pot. (If the water boils, many bubbles arise, but these are steam bubbles.)

If we have a box in which we cannot see anything, we say that the box is empty. After we have drunk all the water in a glass, we say that there

How can you prove that air is really a kind of matter?

The air that occupies the space in the glass prevents the water from pushing up all the way in the glass.

is nothing in the glass. Yet, it is not true that there is nothing in the box and glass — both are full of air. Although we cannot see air, we must not believe that air is nothing at all. Air is matter. Like all matter, it takes up space and has weight.

Lower a drinking glass, mouth downward, into a large jar or pot three-quarters full of water. Note that the water pushes only a little way up into the glass. What keeps the water from rising all the way up into the glass? Something must be taking up the space inside the glass and thereby keeping the water out. It is air that occupies the space in the glass.

Obtain two balloons of the same size. Blow them up to the same size, and tie their necks so that the air will not escape. After tying each balloon, leave about a foot-and-a-half of string free, and tie a loop at the end of each string.

Tie a string around the middle of a yardstick, and suspend it so that it swings freely. Slip the loops at the ends of the strings that are attached to the balloons over the ends of the yardstick, and adjust the balloons so that they balance the yardstick. When the yardstick has stopped swinging, burst one of the balloons with a pin. The other balloon will swing downward. Since both the full balloon and the burst balloon weigh the same, there must be something on the side of the full balloon that pulls the yardstick down on that side. This something is the air in the balloon. This proves that air has weight.

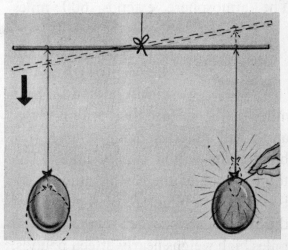

You can actually demonstrate that air has weight.

7

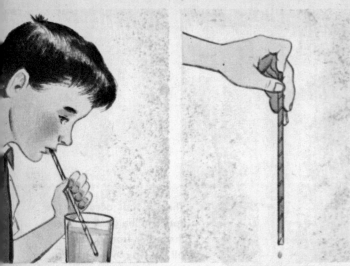
Atmospheric pressure holds water in the straw.

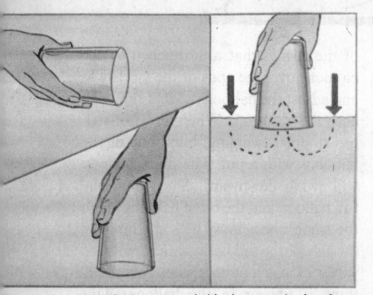
Atmospheric pressure holds the water in the glass.

That means that the atmosphere presses down on every inch of the earth's surface (at sea level) with an average weight of fifteen pounds. We refer to this weight when we speak of atmospheric pressure. But pressure is not only directed downward — it is exerted equally in *all* directions! Total pressure of the air on the body of a man or woman is actually several tons! We are not crushed, however, because the air inside of us, in the water of all our cells, is pushing *outward* with equal pressure.

The earth's atmosphere is divided into several layers. The *troposphere* is the base layer, followed by the *stratosphere*, *ionosphere*, and *exosphere*.

The atmosphere extends 600 miles above the earth's surface. One-quarter of the atmosphere is within one-and-a-half miles of the surface, half within three-and-a-half miles, and ninety-nine one-hundredths within twenty miles. The total weight of the earth's atmosphere is one million billion tons. A column of the atmosphere one inch square and 600 miles high weighs nearly fifteen pounds.

What is atmospheric pressure?

Fill a drinking straw with water, and place your finger tightly over one end. Turn the straw so that the open end points downward.

How can we demonstrate atmospheric pressure?

Some water will run out, but most will remain in the straw. What keeps most of the water from running out? It is the atmospheric pressure that is pressing upward at almost fifteen pounds per square inch.

Run enough water into a sink or large jar so that you can place a glass on its side completely under water. Keeping the glass under water, turn it around so that its mouth points downward. Raise the glass, until all but about half an inch of it is out of the water. The glass remains full of water, even though it is upside down. What keeps the water in the glass? Atmospheric pressure on the surface of the water in the sink or jar pushes water up into the glass. The weight of the air on the surface of the water in the sink or jar is greater than the weight of the water in the glass. Thus the water is held inside the glass at a level higher than the surface of the water outside the glass.

The experiments you just performed are somewhat like one performed by the Italian physicist, Evangelista Torricelli (1608-1647), who was a pupil of Galileo. In the year 1643 he filled a glass tube (closed at one end) with mercury, placed his finger over the open end, and, after turning the tube upside down, placed this end vertically in a small trough of mercury. Once the end of the tube was under the surface of the mercury, he removed his finger—and noted that the mercury in the tube fell only to a measured height of about thirty inches above the surface of the mercury in the trough. Torricelli properly concluded from this that the weight of the air sustained the mercury in the tube, the height of the column being in inverse ratio to its specific gravity.

Otto von Guericke (see page 11) shortly thereafter invented a water barometer, which took the form of a vertical tube nearly forty feet long attached to the side of a house. The tube was brass except for a closed glass section at the top. It was filled with water, its lower end beneath the surface of water in a large tub. The water ordinarily reached a height of thirty-four feet in

The first water barometer in Magdeburg (Germany), 1646.

Changes of air pressure are measured by a barometer. A mercurial barometer consists of a column of mercury in a glass tube about 35 inches high. As the pressure of the atmosphere changes, the column of mercury rises and falls. An aneroid barometer consists of a tightly-sealed can from which some air has been removed. A pointer is soldered to a pivot at the top of the can. As the pressure of air changes, the top of the can moves in or out, thus moving the pointer over a scale on which changes in pressure may be read.

ANEROID BAROMETER

MERCURY BAROMETER

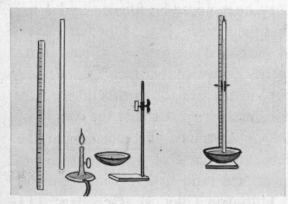

You can make a mercurial barometer in your school laboratory. Obtain a glass tube about 35 inches long. Place one end of the tube into a hot flame, such as that of a Bunsen burner. Twirl the tube around until the end melts and is sealed. When the tube has cooled, fill it to the top with mercury. Also, fill a dessert dish or beaker with mercury. Hold your finger over the open end of the tube and carefully invert it, placing the open end beneath the surface of the mercury in the dish. Place a yardstick alongside the glass tube and clamp both upright. Changes in pressure may be read on the yardstick as the height of the mercury in the tube changes.

the tube, but it alternately rose and fell as the weather caused the barometric pressure to change, and people passing by were able to see this through the glass section.

A siphon is a tube in the form of an inverted U, through which liquids flow over the walls of a container, due to atmospheric pressure. To make a siphon, obtain a rubber or plastic tube, about three feet long and not more than half an inch wide. You will also need two water pails, or other deep vessels. Fill one pail three-quarters full of water, and place it in a sink. Place the other pail on the floor.

How can you make a siphon?

Hold one end of the tube in each hand and completely fill the tube with water from the faucet. Place your fingers over the ends of the tube, so that no water can escape. Quickly place one end well below the surface of the water in the pail in the sink. Let the other end of the tube hang down above the pail on the floor. This end of the tube must be lower than the end in the water. Remove your fingers from both ends of the tube at the same time. You will find that water flows through the tube, over the top of the pail in the sink, and down to the pail on the floor. The operation you have just performed takes some skill, so that you may have to try it more than once, but it is not really difficult.

Why does water flow over the edge of the pail? Because, when you removed your finger from the lower end of the tube, some water fell out, just as it did from the drinking straw in your first experiment on atmospheric pressure.

How to make your own siphon.

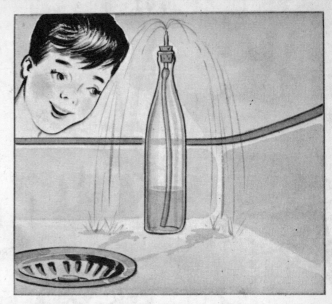

Obtain a cork that fits tightly into the neck of a soda bottle. (A one-hole rubber stopper will work even better than a cork.) Bore a narrow hole through the cork. Into this hole, push the glass tube from an eye dropper. Be sure that the tube fits the hole tightly. If it does not, seal it into the hole with rubber cement, modeling clay, or putty. Using a length of rubber tubing, attach to the wide end of the eye dropper tube a length of glass tubing that reaches nearly to the bottom of the bottle. Fill the bottle about one-fourth full of water. Lower the glass-tube assembly into the bottle and press the cork tightly in. Hold the cork with your fingers, and blow hard into the bottle in order to compress the air within. Quickly point the bottle away from you, and watch a stream of water gush from the tip of the eye dropper tube.

The water that fell out of the tube left an empty space behind it. Atmospheric pressure on the surface of water in the pail pushed water up into the tube to fill the empty space. More water fell out of the bottom of the tube, and was again replaced, due to atmospheric pressure — and the water continued to flow through the siphon tube.

In 1654, a German scientist, Otto von Guericke, amazed everyone by showing how much force could be exerted by the pressure of the atmosphere. He used two iron hemispheres, each of which was about twenty-two inches in diameter. Their rims were

How can you demonstrate the force of air pressure?

carefully ground smooth and covered with grease. He put the rims together, and, with a vacuum pump he had invented, removed the air inside the hollow sphere. So great was the air pressure on the outside that it took sixteen horses, eight on each side, to pull the hemispheres apart.

You can perform an experiment like that of von Guericke. You will need two plungers of the kind that are used to force water through drains. You will also need a friend to help you. Thoroughly wet both plungers. Ask your friend to sit in a chair and hold the

plunger handle between his knees, the rubber cup upward. Place the cup of your plunger upon the other one, and slowly and carefully push down until most of the air has been expelled from the plunger cups. Now, each of you grasp a handle, and see how difficult it is to pull the plungers apart.

If you have only one plunger, place it on a smooth wet surface, and push down hard. You will see how strongly you have to pull in order to pull it free. All the force holding the plunger to the surface is due to atmospheric pressure.

How does atmospheric pressure help us breathe?

When we take a breath, air enters our lungs. People usually say that we "draw" air into our lungs, but this is not an accurate way to describe what happens. Let us see how we breathe. Our lungs are two large sacs of membrane suspended within the cage of our ribs. The lungs have no muscles, and therefore we have no direct control over them. Below our lungs is a large curved muscle, called the *diaphragm*. To take a breath, we pull the top of this muscle downward. Doing this raises our ribs

It took sixteen horses, eight on each side, to pull the steel spheres apart after the German scientist Otto von Guericke had removed the air between the spheres. This occurred in 1654 in Magdeburg. Try to separate two plungers and you will see how difficult it can be.

and makes more room within the rib cage. The lungs now have room to expand. The air pressure outside the lungs is greater than the air pressure within the lungs, so air is pushed into the lungs from outside our body. This is the act of inhaling.

To exhale, we relax the diaphragm, thereby lowering the rib cage, which presses the air out of the lungs.

To make a model of our breathing apparatus, we need a bell jar — a bell-shaped glass that is open at the bottom. We also need a one-hole rubber stopper that will fit the neck of the bell jar,

a glass tube in the shape of a Y, two small balloons, and a large thin piece of rubber.

Place the stopper in the mouth of the jar. Tie the two balloons to the ends of the arms of the Y-tube. Put the other end of the Y-tube into the hole in the stopper, doing so by way of the bottom of the bell jar. Tie the large piece of rubber around the bottom of the bell jar.

The large piece of rubber represents the diaphragm. The upper part of the Y-tube represents the trachea, the arms represent the bronchial tubes, and the balloons represent the lungs. By pulling

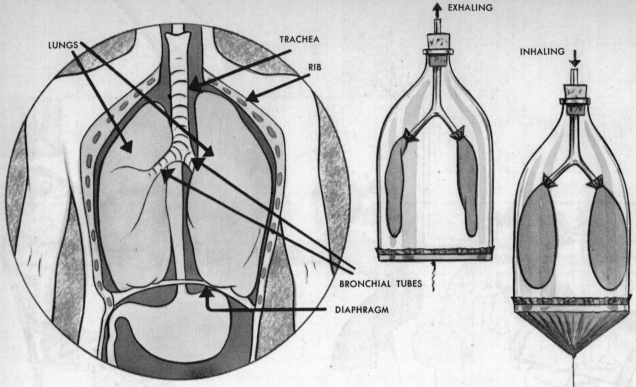

LUNGS

TRACHEA

RIB

EXHALING

INHALING

BRONCHIAL TUBES

DIAPHRAGM

How we breathe (at left) and how you can simulate the process of breathing. Since a bell jar is expensive and hard to obtain, this experiment should be done in your school laboratory where bell jars are standard equipment.

down on the rubber diaphragm, you simulate the act of inhaling. Then, by pushing upward on the diaphragm, you simulate exhaling.

A Cartesian diver is a toy that depends on two principles: The first is that air is elastic, and the second is that air is lighter than water. You can easily prove that air is elastic by holding a finger tightly over the outlet of a tire pump. Push the plunger in, and suddenly let go. The plunger springs back as if it had been pushed into rubber, which, as you know, is very elastic.

How can you make Cartesian divers?

That air is lighter than water is proved by the fact that air bubbles rise in water. Lighter materials rise to the top of heavier ones. Thus, air is lighter than water.

A real Cartesian diver is a tiny figure of a man made of some material that is a little heavier than water. Inside this figure is a small glass tube, closed at one end, and with the open end pointing downward. The whole apparatus is made of materials of such weight that it floats just below the surface of the water. The Cartesian diver is put into a tall jar filled with water to the very top, and covered by a thin piece of rubber. When you press down on the rubber, the water transmits your push to the air in the glass tube inside the diver. The air, being elastic, is compressed, so that it occupies a smaller space. The result is that the air is less able to hold up the diver, which sinks toward the bottom of the jar. By giving the rubber just the right amount of push, you can make the diver rise and sink, or float at any level you wish.

14

It is quite difficult to make a real Cartesian diver, but we can have much fun with substitute divers. Our divers will be paper matches cut in half, the half with the matchheads attached being used. We place three or four of our divers into a bottle with a very thin neck, one over which you can easily place your thumb. Fill the bottle with water to the very top. The half matches will float because of air within the fibers of the paper.

Put your thumb over the top of the bottle, and press downward. This will compress the air in the half matches, and their heavy heads will pull them down to the bottom. When you release the pressure of your thumb, the divers will rise. With a little practice, you can make your divers sink and rise and float at whatever level you wish.

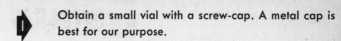 Obtain a small vial with a screw-cap. A metal cap is best for our purpose.

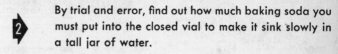 By trial and error, find out how much baking soda you must put into the closed vial to make it sink slowly in a tall jar of water.

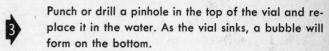 Punch or drill a pinhole in the top of the vial and replace it in the water. As the vial sinks, a bubble will form on the bottom.

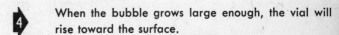 When the bubble grows large enough, the vial will rise toward the surface.

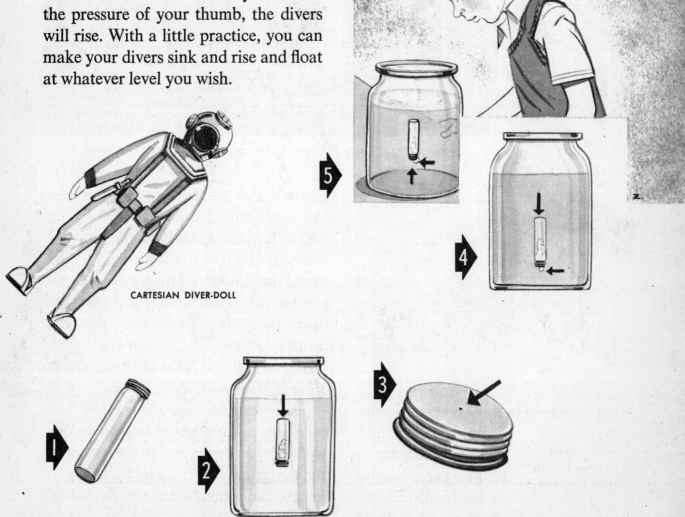 As the vial rises, most of the bubble will be detached, and the vial will sink again. This rising and sinking will be repeated over and over.

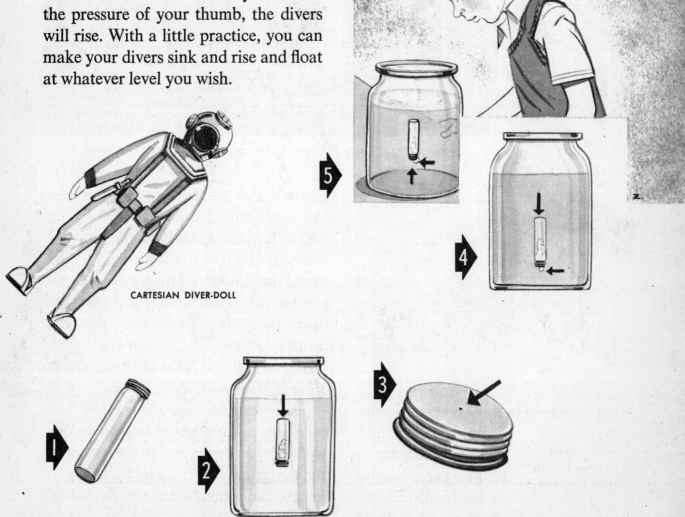

CARTESIAN DIVER-DOLL

MELTING ICE
BECOMES WATER

BOILING WATER
BECOMES STEAM

DROPS OF WATER
FORM ON THE SPOON

Because ice is lighter than water, it floats. This permits life to go on in a frozen pond.

Water can exist in three different forms, or *states:* solid, liquid, and gas. Put three or four ice cubes in a tea kettle, and put the kettle over a small flame on a stove.

Why aren't fishes frozen in winter ice?

Leave the lid off the kettle, so that you can watch what happens inside. As the ice is heated, it melts and becomes water; it changes from the solid to the liquid state. When all the ice has melted, put the lid on the kettle, and turn the flame up higher. Make sure that the spout is pointing away from you. Soon, the water will boil. You will see steam in front of the spout. Steam is made up of little droplets of water. Look closely at the space just in front of the spout. You will see what looks like an empty space, but the space is taken up by water vapor, which is invisible, because it is colorless. Water vapor is water in the state of a gas. To prove that water vapor is a form of water, wrap a towel around the handle of a tablespoon, and hold the bowl of the spoon in the seemingly empty space in front of the spout. You will see drops of water form on the spoon. If you put these drops of water into the freezer of a refrigerator, they would freeze and become ice.

Water is an unusual substance, because, unlike most other substances, it is lighter in its solid than its liquid state. Ice is lighter than water. When water is cooled to within a few degrees of its freezing point, it suddenly begins to become lighter. It continues to become lighter until it freezes. The fact that ice is lighter is important to all fish, plants, and other forms of life that live in water that freezes in winter. When a pond, lake, or river freezes, the ice floats. This leaves water below, in which fish, water plants, and other living things continue to live almost as they did before the ice formed. If ice were heavier than water, a body of water would freeze from the bottom upward. The water plants would freeze and die. The fish would have shallower and shallower water in which to swim, as the level of ice rose. Finally, the fish would be frozen into the ice as the last water, at the surface, froze. You

have surely seen ice cubes floating in cool drinks. The fact that the ice floats proves it is lighter than water.

You can demonstrate why ice is lighter than water by means **Why is ice lighter than water?** of the following experiment. Obtain a small screw-cap bottle with a narrow neck and wide shoulders. Fill the bottle to the very top with water, and screw the cap on tightly. Put about two dozen ice cubes into a pail. Add three glassfuls of water. Also add a generous handful of salt. Place the screw-cap bottle into the ice, water mixture, and salt. Stir the mixture frequently. After about fifteen minutes, or more, the water in the bottle will freeze and the bottle will break. If the ice melts before the water in the bottle freezes, add more ice and a little more salt.

Why did the bottle break? It broke because when the water in the bottle froze, it expanded. The ice expanded to take up more room than the water. Since the ice took up more room, it could no longer fit into the bottle, and the force of its expansion broke the bottle.

Suppose you had another bottle the same size as the one that broke, and

When water freezes, it expands.
Ice takes more room than water.

suppose that there were some way to put the ice into this bottle. Since the ice takes up more room than the water, you would have some ice left over. Now, if you let the ice in the bottle melt, the water from the melted ice would not fill the bottle. This is true because some of the water originally in the first bottle made up the ice you couldn't put into the second bottle. You can easily see that an amount of water that only partly fills a bottle will weigh less than an amount that completely fills the bottle. The water from the melted ice only partly filled the bottle. This shows that a bottle of ice weighs less than a bottle of water. So, ice weighs less than water.

We learned that water vapor is water in the state of a gas.

How can you take water out of air?

It is not necessary to boil water in order to cause it to become water vapor. At the surface of any body of water, some water is almost always leaving the surface and passing into the air in the form of water vapor. There are tons and tons of water vapor in the atmosphere. Warm air can contain more water vapor than cool air. Air can be cooled to a point at which it can no longer hold all the water vapor it contains. When this happens, the water vapor forms droplets of water. Clouds are made up of droplets of water that has formed from water vapor; so is fog. If clouds are cooled further, their droplets of water form big drops that fall as rain.

Another form in which water vapor leaves the air is dew. At night, leaves, grass, and stones cool more quickly than the air. Air passing over these cool objects is, in its turn, cooled. The cool air cannot hold its water vapor, which leaves the air to form the dew drops so familiar to anyone who goes out early on a summer morning. The temperature at which water vapor becomes water is called the *dew point*.

Nature's water cycle, evaporation, condensation, and precipitation, repeats itself endlessly.

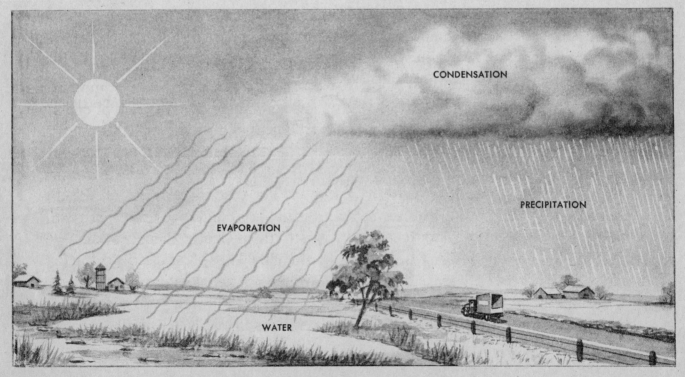

CONDENSATION

PRECIPITATION

EVAPORATION

WATER

As there is always some moisture in the air, the jar will always be moist after the temperature has reached the dew point.

Let us form dew and measure the dew point in the following manner. Put water and some ice cubes into a shiny tin can. Just before putting a thermometer into the can, read the temperature. This is the temperature of the air. Stir the ice and water slowly. Watch the outside of the can carefully. When you see drops of water begin to form on the can, read the thermometer. This temperature is the dew point, and is the temperature of air that is touching the can. Note that this temperature is lower than the temperature of the surrounding air.

Why does an electric fan cool us?

Everyone knows that air from an electric fan feels cool on a hot day. We usually take it for granted that the fan is blowing cool air. But if you stop to think about it, you will realize that the air the fan is blowing upon you is the same air that makes you feel uncomfortably warm. Why, then, does this blast of warm air make you feel cool?

When we heat water so that it turns into water vapor, we say we are *evapo-*

rating the water. In order to evaporate, the water takes up some of the heat that we apply. Suppose you heat a spoon, and then drop some warm water into it. If the spoon is hot enough, the water will sizzle and dance about in the bowl of the spoon — and evaporate. When this has happened, the spoon will be much cooler. The main reason for this is that the spoon used up much heat in evaporating the water. Thus, you can see that evaporation is a cooling process.

On hot days you perspire, and your perspiration gathers in small drops on your skin, where it slowly evaporates. When a blast of air from a fan strikes

Evaporation is a cooling process.

the perspiration, the rate of evaporation is greatly increased. Since evaporation is a cooling process, the rate of cooling is increased, and the air from the fan causes you to feel cool.

Read the temperature on a thermometer. Put two or three layers of moistened cleansing tissue around the bulb of the thermometer. Place the thermometer in the blast of air of an electric fan. Watch the temperature go down, as evaporation of water from the tissue cools the thermometer's bulb.

THE "MAGIC" BALLOON

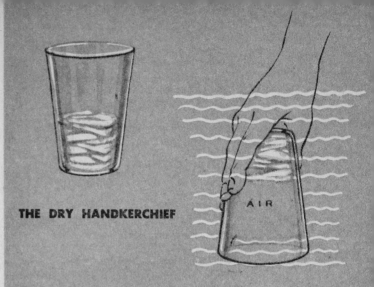

THE DRY HANDKERCHIEF

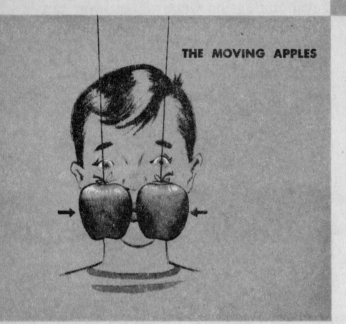

THE MOVING APPLES

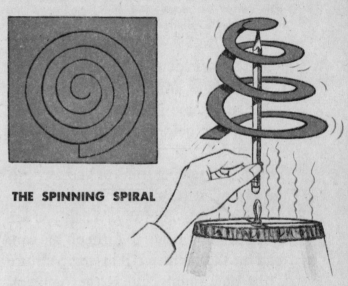

THE SPINNING SPIRAL

THE "MAGIC" BALLOON

Place a soda bottle in a bowl of ice cubes or cracked ice. After a few minutes, when the bottle has become cold, slip a deflated balloon over the neck of the bottle. Remove the bottle from the ice and wait about five minutes until the bottle returns to room temperature. Now place the bottle in a bowl of hot water. The balloon will become inflated as the heat expands the air within the bottle.

THE DRY HANDKERCHIEF

Push a handkerchief firmly into the lower half of a drinking glass. Be sure that the handkerchief will not fall out when the glass is turned upside down. Fill a large pot or a sink with water. Push the glass, open end down, below the surface of the water. The handkerchief will remain dry because the air in the glass occupies space and therefore prevents the water from rising into the glass.

THE MOVING APPLES

Suspend two apples so that they hang about half an inch apart. When they hang absolutely still, place your mouth close to the space between the apples and blow hard. Instead of flying apart, the apples will move closer together. Whenever air moves fast, its pressure is lowered. With the pressure between the apples lessened, the normal air pressure on the rest of the apples' surfaces pushes them together.

THE SPINNING SPIRAL

Cut a spiral out of a piece of paper. Balance your spiral on the point of a pencil. To do this, you may have to press the paper down lightly upon the pencil point, but do not press hard enough to make a hole in the paper. Hold the spiral over a lighted electric bulb or over the shade of a lighted lamp. Your spiral will spin around the pencil because the rising warm air pushes the spiral around.

THE FALLING PAPER

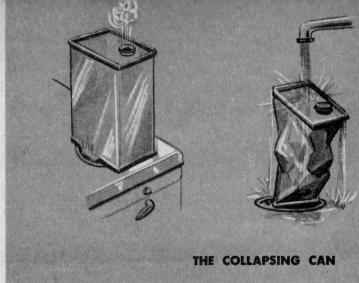

THE COLLAPSING CAN

THE FLOATING EGG

THE SWIMMING FISH

THE FALLING PAPER

Crumple a sheet of paper tightly into a wad. Hold the paper wad and a flat sheet of paper at the same height above your head. Hold the sheet parallel to the floor. Let go of both pieces of paper at the same moment. The paper wad will strike the floor before the sheet. The rounded surface of the paper wad offers less resistance to the air than the flat paper sheet. Streamlined airplanes, automobiles, and trains have rounded surfaces so as to offer less resistance to the air they move through.

THE COLLAPSING CAN

Obtain a gallon can with a screw-cap that fits tightly. Pour a glass of water into the can. Heat the can on a gas range until steam pours from the opening. Turn off the heat. Using a potholder, quickly place the can in the sink and screw the cap on tightly. Run cold water over the can. The can will buckle and collapse. The steam drove the air out of the can, and when, in the cooled can, the steam condensed to water, a partial vacuum was formed. As a result, the greater air pressure on the outside crushed the can.

THE FLOATING EGG

Place an egg into a tall glass of water, and watch it sink to the bottom. Add a tablespoon of salt to the water and carefully stir it until the salt dissolves. By the time you have finished this operation, the egg will be floating at the surface of the water. (If not, add more salt.) A volume of salt water equal to the volume of the egg weighs more than the egg and therefore pushes the egg to the surface.

THE SWIMMING FISH

Cut a piece of cardboard or stiff paper into the shape of a fish. Cut into the tail of the fish a channel that ends in a hole about one-eighth of an inch in diameter. Suspend a drop of oil in this hole. Place the fish on the surface of a panful of water. The fish will move forward under its own power because the oil lessens the surface tension behind the fish. (You can use a piece of soap or camphor in place of the oil.)

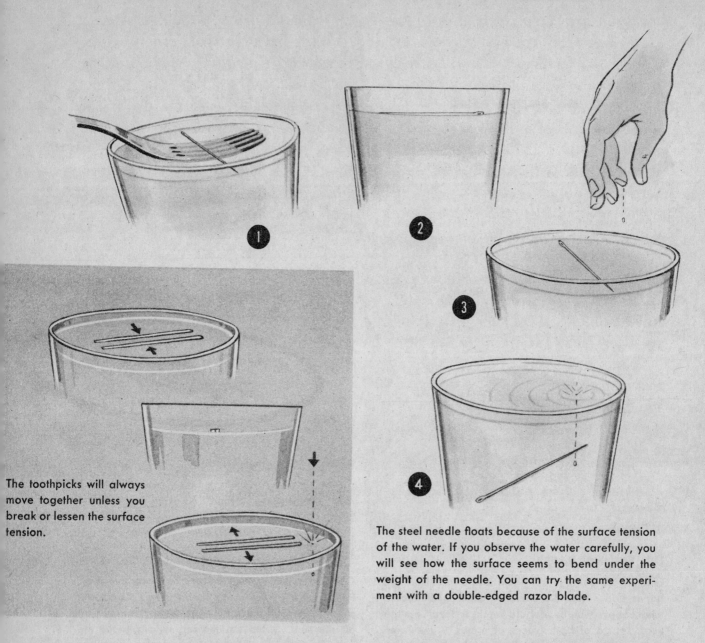

The toothpicks will always move together unless you break or lessen the surface tension.

The steel needle floats because of the surface tension of the water. If you observe the water carefully, you will see how the surface seems to bend under the weight of the needle. You can try the same experiment with a double-edged razor blade.

Everyone knows that steel will not float.

How can you make steel float? Steel is nearly eight times as heavy as water. Yet it is easy to make a piece of steel float. Place a sewing needle upon the tines of a fork. Lower the fork into a glass filled with water. The needle will float. The needle is made of steel. Why does it float?

Water is made up of tiny particles called *molecules*. The molecules attract each other like tiny magnets. The mole-cules at the surface of a liquid attract each other strongly enough to be able to support small weights, such as a needle. This molecular attraction at the surface of liquids is called *surface tension*.

When you have floated the needle, obtain some soap powder or detergent powder. Soap and detergent clean because they lessen the surface tension of water, and cause oils and greases to form tiny particles that can be washed away. Drop just one single grain of soap powder or detergent into the glass containing the floating needle. Watch the needle immediately sink, as the surface tension is lessened.

The surface of a liquid is actually in a state of tension; that is, it exists as if it were being pulled tight. Place two toothpicks about one-eighth of an inch apart, side by side, in a glass of water. They will move together because the surface of the water is a little higher at the sides of the glass. It is as though you placed two iron pipes near the middle of a blanket that was being held taut by its edges. The pipes would roll together.

Add a few grains of soap powder or detergent to the water, and watch the toothpicks fly apart, as the surface tension is lessened.

up behind a dam. In the dam are one or more openings that lead to a long pipe called a *penstock*. Water from behind the dam flows downward through the penstock and comes out the bottom of this long pipe with great force because of the difference in water elevation. At the lower opening of the penstock is a *turbine,* a great wheel with blades radiating outward from its center. Water flows through the penstock and strikes the blades of the turbine, causing the wheel to turn rapidly. The axle of the turbine runs to an electric generator, which it turns. In this way, water generates electricity.

A water wheel also depends upon difference in water elevation. Push a knitting needle through the exact center of a cork. Stick half a dozen ink pens

Water is a fairly heavy substance. You

How does water help to generate electricity?

will prove this for yourself, if you try to lift a bucket filled with water. Water is put to work by first penning it

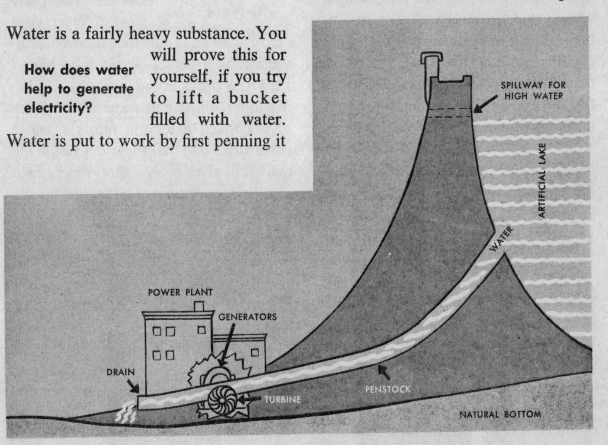

Water is put to work to help create electricity.

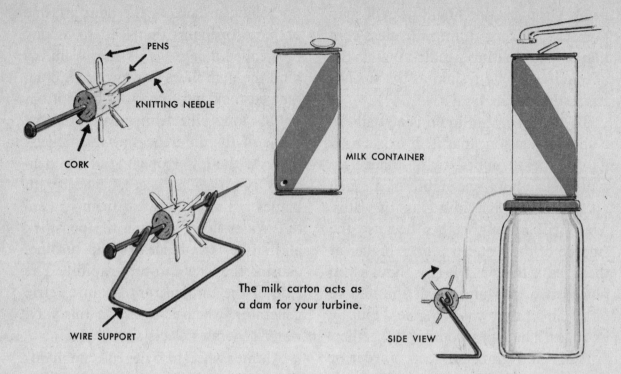

PENS

KNITTING NEEDLE

CORK

MILK CONTAINER

WIRE SUPPORT

The milk carton acts as a dam for your turbine.

SIDE VIEW

(nibs) into the outside of the cork in a circle. Place the knitting needle on a wire cradle made from a coat hanger. This is your water wheel, a crude turbine. Punch a small hole near the bottom of a milk carton. Place the carton beneath a faucet in a sink, and arrange the turbine so that water running out of the hole in the carton strikes the pens. Your water wheel will spin rapidly, as long as water continues to shoot out of the carton, which is acting as the dam.

How does water rise to the tops of trees?

In the Sequoia National Park in California, some of the trees are thirty stories tall. Water rises from their roots to their tops. How does this take place? Put a few drops of red, or green, or blue ink into a glassful of water. Put a piece of uncooked macaroni into the water vertically. Note that the water inside the macaroni rises higher than the surface of the water outside. The reason for the

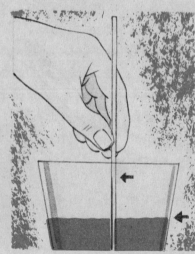

The water inside the macaroni rises higher than the surface of the water outside.

Capillary action makes the water rise from the roots of plants to the highest leaves.

rise of water inside the tube of macaroni is that the water molecules are attracted to the sides of the tube, and "creep" up the sides. The rise of liquids in thin tubes is called *capillary action*. The thinner the tube, the higher the rise.

Inside all woody plants there are thousands of tubes. So small is the diameter of each tube that it is hard to see it with the naked eye. It is capillary action in these tubes that raises water to the tops of plants, including the tallest trees.

Put a freshly-cut celery stalk into colored water. After a few hours, note that the leaves are colored by the water that has risen through the stalk by capillary action.

Sound

The world is full of sound. In the streets of a busy town, we hear the honking of auto horns, the rumble of trucks, the screech of brakes, shouts, thumps, clangs, and dozens of other sounds you can easily name. Indoor sounds are familiar to all: footsteps on the floor, the thud of closing doors, people talking, music and voice from television or radio, the rattle of dishes, silverware, and kitchen utensils. In the country, you may hear the songs of birds, cawing of crows, lowing of cattle, the buzz-

What is sound?

ing of insects, or the rustle of leaves as a breeze blows through the trees. Even in the quietest night, you can hear your own breathing. There is no time when you are awake that you cannot hear sounds.

When an object vibrates — moves rapidly back and forth — sound is produced.

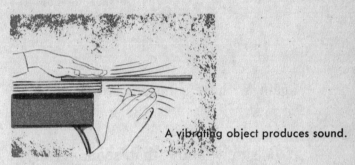
A vibrating object produces sound.

Obtain a ruler or a wooden lath. Place it on a table, so that about two-thirds of the ruler projects over the edge of the table. Hold the ruler firmly with the palm of one hand. Pull the free end of the ruler down about an inch, and then suddenly let go. Do you see the ruler vibrate at the same time you hear the deep hum it makes? When it stops vibrating, place your ear close to the ruler. Now, you hear no sound coming from the ruler. Clearly then, the vibration of the ruler had something to do with the sound it made.

Hold a dinner fork close to your ear, and listen carefully. No sound comes from the fork. Strike the edge of the fork against a table or some other hard object. Note the prongs' blurry appearance caused by their rapid vibration. Again, strike the fork against the table, and quickly bring the fork close to your ear. You will easily hear the sound coming from the rapidly-moving prongs. So,

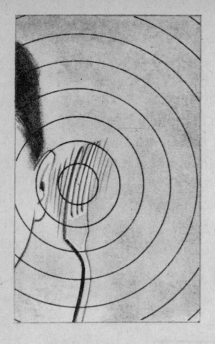

No sound will come from the tines of a dinner fork unless you make the prongs vibrate.

again, we have connected vibration and sound.

How does sound travel? You surely know that sound always travels from the source of the sound. A friend shouts to you, and you know that the sound of his voice travels from his throat to your ears. You hear the sound of an airplane's engine because sound travels from the engine to you. You probably can name a hundred instances in your daily experience in which sound travels from its source to your ears. Even the sound of your own voice has to travel from your vocal cords to your ears.

Can we perform an experiment that will show us something about how sound travels? We can, if we use a bell jar. The bell jar rests, open side down, on a circular metal plate that has a hole in its center. A rubber tube runs from this hole to a pump that can pull air out of the bell jar.

We set an alarm clock to go off in one minute, and place the clock on a sponge on the metal plate. We coat the rim of the bell jar with grease, such as petroleum jelly, before placing it on the metal plate. The grease prevents air from leaking in or out of the bell jar. Soon, we clearly hear the clock ring.

We remove the bell jar, wind the alarm, set it to go off in five minutes, and replace the clock, sponge, and bell jar on the metal plate. Now, we start the pump pulling air out of the bell jar. When, at the end of five minutes, the alarm rings, we can barely hear it. What has happened? We guess that lack of air in the bell jar has diminished the amount of sound that the alarm produces. Our guess is right. If all the air were pumped out of the bell jar, we would not hear the alarm at all — because the alarm would make no sound whatever. From this experiment we can

conclude that air was needed for the vibrations of the alarm to travel in the form of sound. The air is called the *medium* in which the sound traveled. The word "medium" comes from the Latin word *medius,* which means "middle." The air served as a middle, or go-between, that conducted the vibrations from the bell to your ear, so that you heard them as sound.

We know that air is quite a satisfactory medium for the

What is the best medium for sound to travel through?

travel of sound, because, except when we are swimming or in the bathtub, sounds always reach our ears through air. Air is a mixture of several gases, so we can say that gases are a

satisfactory medium for sound. Liquids are a better medium than gases; and solids are even better than liquids.

Next time you are swimming, try this experiment. Ask a friend to stand about fifty feet from you and to strike two medium-sized rocks together. Put your head under water, and ask your friend

Water is better than air as a conductor of sound.

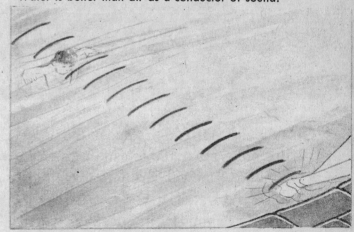

to strike the rocks together, again, this time beneath the surface of the water. You will notice that the sound of the striking rocks is louder under water. This shows that water is better than air as a medium for carrying sound.

To learn how well solids conduct

A bell jar is expensive. For home experimentation, use instead a large peanut butter jar.

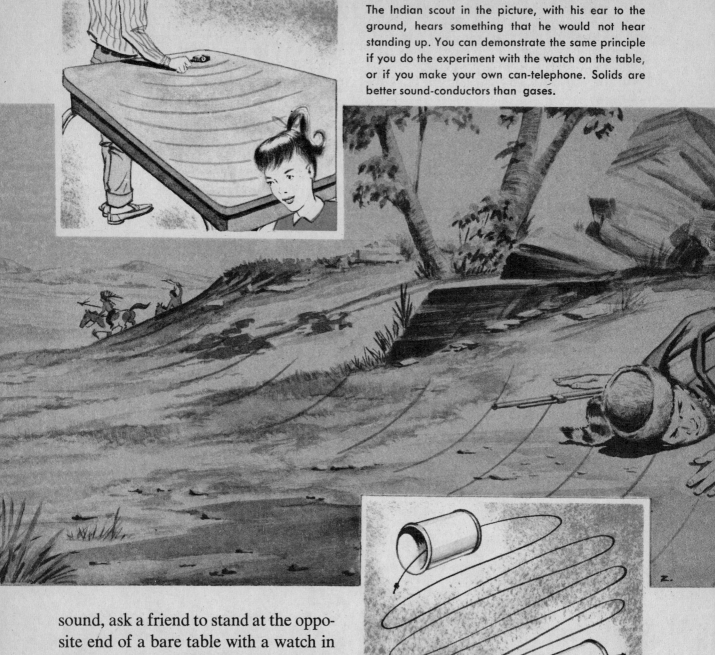

sound, ask a friend to stand at the opposite end of a bare table with a watch in his hand. You will hardly hear the ticking of the watch, if you hear it at all. Now, have your friend place the watch on his end of the table while you put an ear to the top of your end of the table. You will hear the watch ticking quite clearly. This shows that the table which is solid, is a better sound-conducting medium than air, which is gas.

Another experiment that shows that solids conduct sound better than gases is this: Thread a length of stout string, about thirty feet long, through a hole in the bottom of each of two empty tin cans. Now, tie thick knots at the ends of the string so that they will not slip back through the holes. Ask a friend to take one of the cans and walk away from you until the string is taut. Ask him to speak in a very low voice, so that you can barely hear him. Then ask him to speak in the same level of voice into his tin can, while you hold yours to your ear. Now, you will hear his voice more loudly, for the string conducts sound better than air does.

We have learned that sound must have **What are sound waves?** a medium in which to travel. We still have to learn in what form sound travels through the medium. The vibrating prongs of a tuning fork produce sound. Let us concentrate on the action of one prong. As the prong moves in one direction, it compresses the air particles in front of it. Then, the prong swings in the opposite direction, and the space that it just occupied is nearly empty of air particles. The surrounding air particles begin to crowd into the partly-empty space, but the prong, swinging forward again, compresses them once more. This process of compressing and rarefying the air around the prong continues as long as the prong vibrates.

The compressed particles of air are pushed against those a little farther away from the prong. This push, or *impulse*, moves farther and farther outward, compressing air particles as it travels. Following behind the compression is a space of rarefied air. Thus, the vibrating prong sends through the air a continual series of alternating compressions and rarefactions. Each pair of compressions and rarefactions makes up one *sound wave*. Sound waves travel outward from a vibrating object like a series of expanding soap bubbles, each one inside the one moving ahead of it.

Scientists have very fast cameras with which they can photograph sound waves. We do not have such a camera, but we can perform experiments that will give us an idea of how sound waves travel.

Run four or five inches of water into a bathtub, washbowl, or kitchen sink. You will need a light above the water, and the ceiling light will do very well.

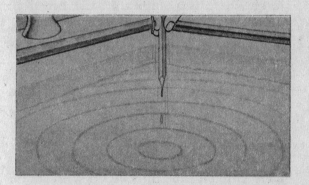

Sharply tap the center of the water with a pencil. Do you see, on the bottom, shadows of a series of rings moving outward from the place where you tapped the water? The rings are crests of water waves.

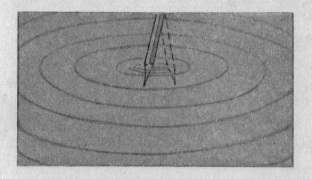

Now dip the pencil into the center of the water. Wag the pencil back and forth rapidly; that is, make the pencil vibrate. You again produce a series of expanding circular water waves that move outward from the pencil, each circle inside the one moving ahead of it. The shadows of the waves are what you would see if you could slice a series of sound waves in half and then look at the cut edges.

It is important to understand that sound waves are not made up of particles of air that move outward from the vibrating object. It is only the push, or impulse, that moves.

From a piece of wood shave half a dozen chips no more than half an inch long. Drop the chips into the water in several locations. Use the pencil to produce more water waves, and note that although the chips may move about a bit, their main motion is to bob up and down as the waves pass them by. If the waves had been made up of water moving outward from the pencil, they would have carried the chips along with them; but they did not. This fact shows us that water waves are simply up-and-down motions that travel along the surface of the water. Knowing this helps us to understand that sound waves are simply pushes that compress and rarefy the air as they travel outward from a vibrating object.

Another experiment that will help you to understand the idea of a moving impulse is the following. Place six coins in a straight row on a smooth table top. Place a seventh coin a half inch behind the row. With a flip of your finger against the seventh coin, cause it to slide along the table and strike the coin at the rear of the row. You will see that the front coin suddenly moves forward away from the row. What moved the front coin? The push you gave the seventh coin traveled all along the row and moved the front coin forward. The other coins remained in place. In much the same way, particles of air remain in place as the push, or impulse, of a sound wave moves through them.

Once again, sharply tap the center of the water. Observe the wave shadows carefully. Note that when they reach the sides of the container, they bounce back

What is an echo?

If you imagine the coins to be particles of air, you can demonstrate how they remain in place as the impulse of a sound wave moves through them.

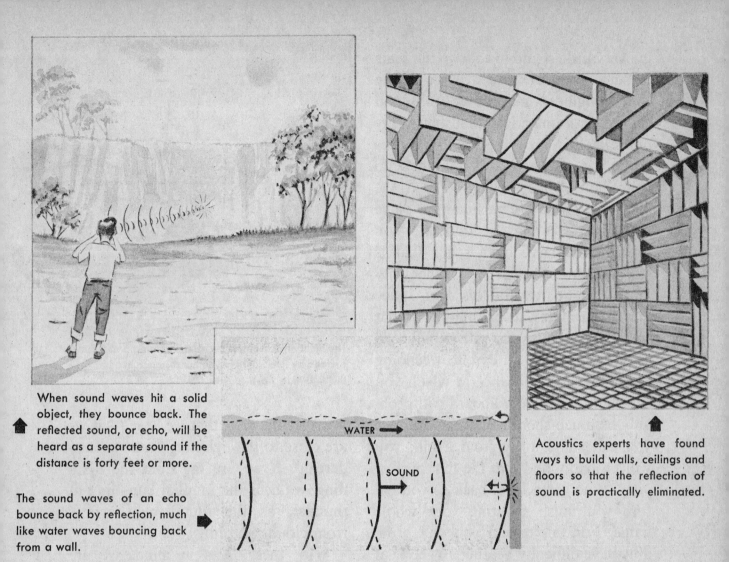

When sound waves hit a solid object, they bounce back. The reflected sound, or echo, will be heard as a separate sound if the distance is forty feet or more.

The sound waves of an echo bounce back by reflection, much like water waves bouncing back from a wall.

WATER

SOUND

Acoustics experts have found ways to build walls, ceilings and floors so that the reflection of sound is practically eliminated.

toward the center. When waves bounce in this manner, they are said to be *reflected*. You are familiar with the reflection of light. The reflection of sound waves from objects they strike is almost exactly the same as the reflection of light from shiny objects. A reflected sound is an *echo*.

If you are in the country, and if you shout your name toward a steep grassy hill or toward the foot of a cliff, the sound of your voice will travel to the hill or cliff and then reflect back as an echo, as though someone in front of you were calling you.

If you shout toward a thickly wooded hill, you will probably hear no echo at all, or only a faint one. The reason for this is that the sound of your voice will strike the leaves, twigs, and branches of the trees. As a result, the sound waves will be reflected at the hundreds of different angles toward which the surfaces of the leaves, twigs, and branches are facing. Only a few surfaces will reflect sound back to you, and usually these are too few to produce an echo loud enough to be heard.

It is interesting to know that sound engineers who want to diminish echoes in theaters copy the manner in which the trees on the wooded hill diminished the echo of your voice. The engineers may build the walls and ceiling of the theater with rippled surfaces, so that sound is reflected at many angles, allowing very little sound to echo to the seats or stage or movie screen. Or else, the sound engineers may cover walls and ceiling with materials that have tiny holes in their surfaces. Sound bounces around in the holes, unable to echo from the walls and ceiling.

If you live in a city, finding a place to hear echoes may be difficult. You must find a large open space that is shielded from traffic and other city noises. At one end of this open space must be a high wall or some other flat surface. An empty lot with a billboard at one end makes an excellent echoing place. Since the distance at which you can stand from the billboard will probably be much shorter than the distance you can stand away from a hill, you will probably find that the first part of your name has echoed back to you before you finish shouting your whole name. For this reason you will probably have difficulty hearing any echo at all. To remedy this situation, shout a short syllable, such as *ba,* or else clap your hands. These sounds will echo clearly.

Sound travels approximately 1,100 feet

How can you measure distance with sound?

per second in air that has a temperature of 70° Fahrenheit. We can use this fact to measure distance. Thunder is sound echoing from cloud to cloud and from cloud to earth. The source of thunder is a lightning flash — a giant electric spark that suddenly and intensely heats the air through which it passes. The heated air expands so rapidly that it gives the neighboring air a powerful push. This push travels as a

The number of seconds between lightning and thunder divided by five will give you the distance in miles from the lightning flash to you.

great sound wave that we hear — if we are close to the lightning — as a thunderclap. If we are far from the lightning, we hear the familiar rumbling of thunder, as the thunderclap echoes from clouds and hills.

With these facts in mind, we are ready to use sound to measure distance. We have to wait for a thunderstorm, and we need a watch with a second hand. When we see a flash of lightning, we note the exact time according to the second hand of the watch. Light travels so fast — 186,000 miles per second — that we can ignore the time it takes light to travel from the lightning flash to our watch. Having timed the moment at which the lightning flashed, we keep our eyes on the watch's second hand to learn how many seconds it will take the first sound of thunder to reach our ears. Since we know that sound travels approximately 1,100 feet per second, we multiply by 1,100 the number of seconds between the lightning flash and the first sound of thunder. This gives the distance in feet from us to the lightning flash. Suppose it took five seconds for the sound of thunder to reach us. We multiply 5 by 1,100 and obtain 5,500, the number of feet from us to the lightning flash. Since 1,100 feet are roughly one-fifth of a mile, we may find the distance of the lightning in miles by dividing the number of seconds by 5. Using the five seconds in the foregoing example, we divide them by 5, and the result is 1; that is, one mile. Since there are 5,280 feet in a mile, and since we found the lightning to be 5,500 feet distant, we can see that our measurement of distance by means of sound was fairly accurate.

How do stringed instruments produce sound? Guitar, banjo, and zither strings are plucked with the fingers or a pick. Violin and cello strings are stroked with a bow. Piano strings are struck with felt hammers. In whatever manner they are played, the strings are caused to vibrate, and thereby to produce sound. But you know that stringed instruments can produce a great variety of sound. Let us see how they vary their sounds.

Fasten shut the lid of a cigar box by gluing it or by nailing it with thin tacks or brads. Drill or cut six holes in the top of the box. In both these operations, be careful not to split the wood.

Break half a dozen rubber bands, so that you can pull them out into single lengths. Use thumbtacks to fasten one end of each rubber band to one end of the top of the box. Fasten the other end of each rubber band to the other end of the box. If the rubber bands are longer than the top of the box, just make sure that the length of each rubber band between thumbtacks is pulled tight. Space the rubber bands evenly apart. Try to get rubber bands of several different thicknesses, and arrange them in order from thickest to thinnest.

Cut two pieces of cardboard that are two inches wide and three inches long. Then draw three lines half an inch apart down the length of each piece of cardboard, thus dividing it into four half-inch strips. Fold each piece of cardboard along its lines so as to make a triangular strip, as shown in the illustration on this page. Fasten the cardboard triangles with adhesive tape. Slip the triangles under the rubber bands, about an inch from each end of the cigar box. Now you have a stringed musical instrument on which you can play tunes by plucking the rubber bands.

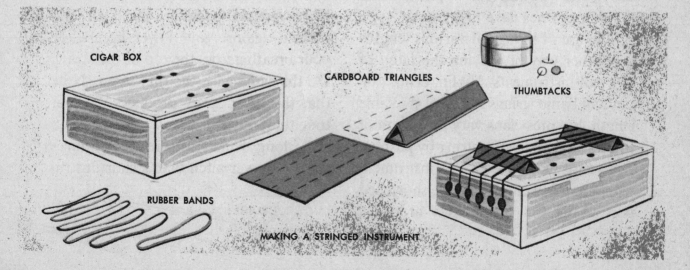

CIGAR BOX   CARDBOARD TRIANGLES   THUMBTACKS   RUBBER BANDS   MAKING A STRINGED INSTRUMENT

As you pluck the rubber bands, note that the thicker ones produce tones of lower pitch than the thin ones. Thick strings on musical instruments are used to produce lower tones, and thin strings to produce higher tones.

Remove the rubber bands from your musical carton, and replace them with six other rubber bands, all of the same thickness. From what we have just learned about the thickness of a musical string and its pitch, we should not be surprised to find that all the strings of our musical carton now have the same pitch. Pluck them and listen. Now, move one of the cardboard triangles, so that it slants across the carton. The result of this move will be to change the

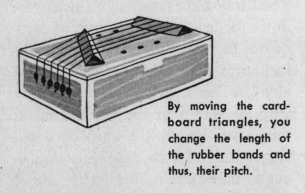

By moving the cardboard triangles, you change the length of the rubber bands and thus, their pitch.

length of those parts of the rubber bands that are between the two triangles. Pluck the rubber bands, and note that the longer ones have low pitch, while the shorter ones have high pitch.

The use of strings of various lengths is another way of varying the pitch of stringed instruments. Violin, cello, guitar, and banjo strings are all of the same length, but musicians vary the length of the vibrating part of a string by pushing it against the neck of the instrument with a finger. Sound from the shortened portion of the string rises in pitch.

Pianos, harps, and harpsichords have strings of different lengths.

Push the triangular piece of cardboard back to its original position. Grasp one of the rubber bands and pull it tighter than its neighbor. Pluck these two rubber bands, one at a time. Note that the tighter one has the higher pitch. Thus, we have a third way in which the pitch of stringed instruments can be varied — by tightening and loosening the strings. You probably have seen a violinist or guitarist tuning his instrument by turning pegs, or keys, at the end of the instrument's neck. In this way, he tightens and loosens strings.

Flutes, piccolos, tubas, saxophones, clarinets, and trombones are among the many wind instruments. When a musician blows into a wind instrument, he causes a column of air inside the instrument to vibrate, and the vibration produces sound waves. A wide wind instrument produces lower tones than a narrow one. A tuba produces lower notes than a flute.

How do wind instruments produce sound?

Obtain a wide drinking straw and a narrow one. Place your finger over one end of the thick straw. Hold the straw in a vertical position, its open end pressed against your lower lip. Below your breath across the top of the straw. Do the same with the thin straw. Note that the thick straw produces a lower tone than the thin straw.

A long wind instrument produces tones of lower pitch than a short instru-

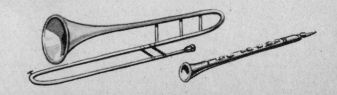

ment. A trombone produces lower notes than a piccolo.

Fill a soda bottle three-quarters full of water. Place a drinking straw in the water. Hold the straw in your right hand and the bottle in your left. Blow across the top of the straw to produce a sound.

The thick straw produces a lower tone than the thin straw.

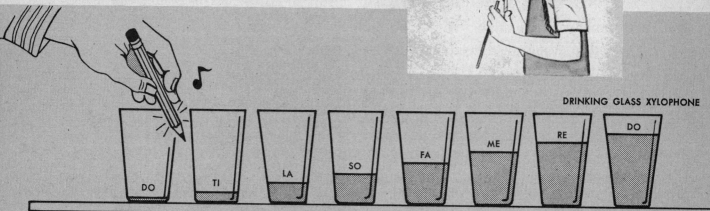

DRINKING GLASS XYLOPHONE

DO TI LA SO FA ME RE DO

Lower the bottle with your left hand, while continuing to blow across the straw. Note that as you lower the bottle, and thereby lengthen the column of air in the straw, the note you are producing lowers in pitch. This is the principle on which the slide trombone works.

THE "WATER TROMBONE"

Drums, cymbals, xylophones, and vibra-

How do percussion instruments produce sound?

phones are percussion instruments. Upon being struck a blow, some part of a percussion instrument vibrates and thereby produces sound. When you strike a drumhead, it vibrates and sets the air inside the drum to vibrating; this magnifies the sound produced. A struck cymbal is simply a vibrating disc of brass. Different tones of a xylophone are produced by pieces

of hardwood of different lengths and thicknesses set vibrating by blows of a small wooden mallet.

Set eight drinking glasses, all of the same size, in a row. Pour half an inch of water into the first glass. Into each succeeding glass pour a little more water than in the glass before it, so that the eighth glass is about three-quarters full. Tap the rim of each glass with a pencil. The differences in the lengths of the air columns in the glasses give them different pitches. Your row of glasses is a sort of xylophone on which you can play tunes.

GALILEO'S
TELESCOPE

Astronomy

What is astronomy? The word *astronomy* comes from two ancient Greek words that mean "to arrange stars." Ancient Greek astronomers made maps of the night sky, and in doing so, they arranged the stars into groups called *constellations*. The Greeks' study of the stars led to the discovery of many facts about other heavenly bodies — the planets, the sun, and the moon. The ancient Greeks had no telescopes, yet they did a remarkable job of describing heavenly bodies. They mapped more than one-third of the constellations we know today, and they described orbits of five of the planets. Other ancient "star-arrangers," or *astronomers,* carried on the work of mapping stars, so that by the second century A.D., the great Egyptian astronomer Ptolemy had mapped more than half the constellations. By that time, he had also worked out a very ingenious system of circular paths to account for the motion of the planets and the apparent motion of the stars.

Astronomy took a giant step forward in 1608 when a Dutch optician by the name of Hans Lippershey invented the telescope. A year later, the Italian astronomer Galileo built his own telescope which soon made possible more precise examination of the heavens.

Today, astronomers are able to study the sun, moon, stars and planets by means of immense optical telescopes and also radio telescopes that can "tune in" on faraway galaxies.

How can you locate the North Star? For more than a thousand years, mariners in the Northern Hemisphere have been guiding their ships by a bright star that is almost exactly in line with the North Pole. This star is called the North Star, the Pole Star, or Polaris. Of course, with the invention of the compass, mariners found less need for the star that enabled them to tell which direction was north. Modern radio-direction-finding has almost eliminated the need for the North Star. But, since this star played so important a part in navigation for so many hundreds of years, let us see whether we can locate it.

On a clear, cloudless night, when the moon is not up, go outdoors and wait a few minutes for your eyes to become

The image labels (within figure): NORTH STAR · BIG DIPPER · LITTLE DIPPER

The Egyptian pyramids, monumental burial tombs of ancient rulers, were also used as points by which stars could be sighted.

Dubhe and Merak, two stars in the Big Dipper, are used to locate the North Star. Regardless of the season of the year, or the location of other stars in the Big Dipper, the Pointer stars always point to the North Star. (See the illustration below.)

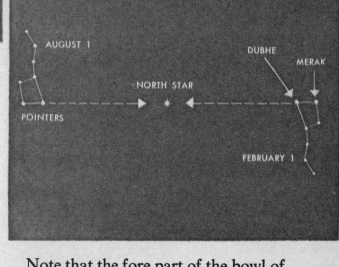

adjusted to the darkness. You must find a location where lighted advertising signs and street lights will not interfere with your seeing.

Look toward the north until you see a group of seven stars that look like points along a dipper with a curved handle. When you have found such a group, or constellation, look around in the same direction for another constellation. It is also in the shape of a dipper, but with the handle curving in the opposite manner from that of the first dipper. The larger of these two is the Big Dipper, and the other is the Little Dipper. They are sometimes called Ursa Major (Big Bear) and Ursa Minor (Little Bear). However, some astronomers consider the Dippers as only parts of Ursa Major and Minor.

Note that the fore part of the bowl of the Big Dipper is made up of two stars. The one at the top of the bowl is called Dubhe, the bottom one, Merak. These two stars are known as the Pointers, because if you draw a line from Merak to Dubhe, and continue the line for a distance equal to about four times the distance between the Pointers, you will arrive at a bright star that is the one we are seeking — the North Star. When you do this, you will probably notice that the North Star is the first star in the handle of the Little Dipper.

No matter what the season of the year, the Pointers always point to the North Star, although, because of the earth's revolution around the sun, the other stars in the Big Dipper seem to shift their positions.

The vast number of stars you see in the sky are all in motion. Some stars are moving thousands of miles per second, but all stars are so far from the earth that they seem to stand still. You can understand this if you think about the fact that a car moving fifty miles per hour seems to whisk rapidly past you, when you are standing by the side of the road; but if you are looking down from a mountain top at a car several miles away and also moving fifty miles per hour, the car now seems to be crawling very slowly. With these facts in mind let us perform our experiment.

How can you use the stars to prove that the earth turns on its axis?

You will need a camera. Any kind of camera will do that has a shutter that can be made to remain open for a time exposure. Load the camera with the most sensitive panchromatic film you can obtain. Your photographic dealer will tell you what kind of film to use.

It is very important now to find a location where there are no interfering lights. A moonless winter night, when the stars are brightest, is best.

Mount your camera on a tripod or some other firm support. Point the camera at the North Star. Try hard to locate the North Star exactly in the center of the camera's finder. Clamp the camera firmly in this position. Set the shutter for a time exposure and click the shutter release. Leave the shutter open for an hour. At the end of this time, be sure to click the shutter release again, to close the shutter.

When the film is developed and a picture is printed from it, you will see many curved white lines against a dark background, and in the center a white spot.

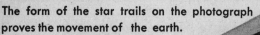
The form of the star trails on the photograph proves the movement of the earth.

If you have successfully centered the North Star, it will be the white spot. The curved lines are the paths of stars. However, we have learned that the stars may be considered as standing still. Therefore, it must have been the camera that turned. But the camera was clamped in one position so that it could not turn. So we are finally led to explain the apparent motion of the stars by saying that it was the earth, upon which the camera was standing, that turned.

Since the camera's shutter was open for one hour, and since we know that the earth makes one complete rotation on its axis in one day — that is, twenty-four hours — we realize that each star path in our picture represents one twenty-fourth of a complete circle.

On a large sheet of paper, draw a circle at least eight inches in diameter. Divide the circle into twelve equal parts, just as a clock face is divided. Alongside each division of the circle, write the name of one of the months where an hour num-

How can you tell the date by the stars?

ber would be on a clock. Start with March in the 12 position; that is, at the top. Keep the months in their usual order, but write them counterclockwise. Mark the center of the circle "North Star." Imagine that the distance on the circle between each month is divided into thirty smaller divisions.

If you are allowed to stay up until midnight on some clear night, take your diagram outdoors. Hold it so that March is at the top. Imagine the diagram in the sky, with the North Star as the center. Note the location of the Big Dipper. Now draw the Big Dipper on your diagram in the same location as you find it in the sky. When you have done this, draw a straight line from the Pointers to the North Star. This line will pass through the circle at a point that will indicate the date on which you are making your observation. Suppose the line passes halfway between the June and July positions on the circle; then it is June 15. Of course, unless you have

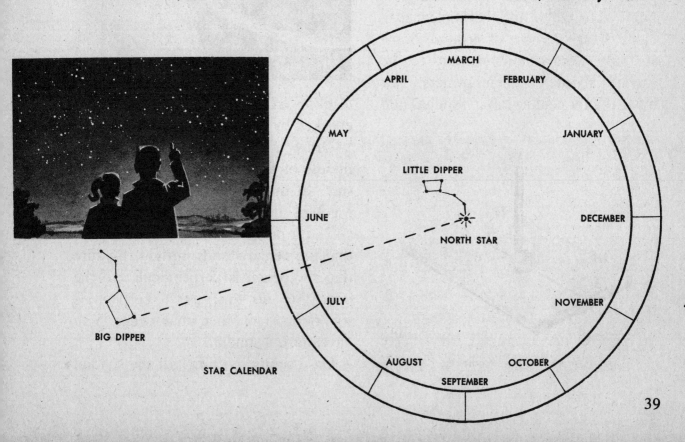

BIG DIPPER

STAR CALENDAR

MARCH

APRIL

FEBRUARY

MAY

JANUARY

LITTLE DIPPER

JUNE

DECEMBER

NORTH STAR

JULY

NOVEMBER

AUGUST

OCTOBER

SEPTEMBER

drawn a very large circle, it will be difficult to estimate thirty divisions between months on the circle. However, you can come within a few days of the exact date. The important thing is to note that on the diagram you have made, on any particular date at midnight, the Pointers are in line with that date on the star calendar.

More than 3,500 years ago, people realized that the sun

How can you tell time by the sun?

could be used to tell the time of day. As a result, they learned how to construct instruments called *sundials*. A shadow cast by the sun pointed to the time of day on a dial that was part of a sundial. The Egyptians made great sundials whose pointers were pyramids and obelisks. Perhaps the largest sundial ever built was constructed at Jaipur, India, in 1724. The pointer of this huge sundial is one-hundred feet high, and the whole instrument covers an acre of ground. Some sundials were small enough to be carried about by their owners. For more than a century after watches and

clocks were in use, their accuracy was checked by sundials.

Draw a straight line through the middle of a board and parallel to one side. In the middle of this line, place a gob of modeling clay. Push the blunt end of a pencil down into the clay, so that the pencil stands upright. Be sure that the pencil is perpendicular to the board; to do this, use a carpenter's square or some other square edge. You have made a sundial.

On a sunny morning, set the sundial

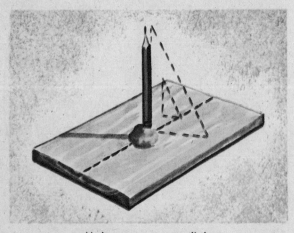

Make your own sundial.

in direct sunlight, with the line on the board running from north to south. You will probably need a magnetic compass to accomplish this positioning. Exactly on each hour, as timed by a watch or clock, make a mark on the board at the exact location of the shadow of the pencil point. Write the hour above the mark. Do not move the board at all.

Leave the board in position. On the next sunny day, you will find that the shadow of the pencil will point to the correct time of day. Leave the board in position for a month or two. Or else, make marks on whatever the board was standing, exactly at the ends of the north-south line on the board. Then, at the end of a month or two, you will be able to replace the board in the exact position in which it was originally.

Having come back to your sundial after a month or two, you will see that it no longer is accurate. Why? As the earth circles around the sun, the sun seems to change the path it makes across the sky. (Of course, the sun is not really moving; the earth's motion makes the sun seem to move.) As the path of the sun changes, so does the accuracy of your sundial, because you made the sundial by means of the sun's path on a particular date. The sundial seemed to be accurate for a few days because the sun changes its path slowly, and you could not immediately note the change.

Obtain a board eight inches square; that

How can you make a more accurate sundial?

is, the board must have each side exactly eight inches long. Draw two diagonals on the board. Where the lines cross is the center of the board. Using a drawing compass, draw a seven-inch circle whose center is the center of the board. Divide half the circle into twelve equal divisions, and, proceeding clockwise, mark them: 6, 7, 8, 9, 10, 11, 12, 1, 2, 3, 4, 5. You have made the dial.

You now have to make the part of the sundial that casts the shadow. This is called the *gnomon* (NO-mon), which is

Greek for "the one that knows." On a piece of wood half an inch thick, draw a triangle that has a base three inches long: thus place a protractor at one end of the base, and mark off an angle equal to your latitude. You can find the latitude of the place in which you live by referring to an atlas. Suppose you live in Chicago, which is at a latitude of 42°; then you mark off an angle of 42°. From the end of the base and through the 42° mark, draw a line eight inches long. From the upper end of this line, draw a straight line to the base to complete the triangle. Now, saw this triangle out of the piece of wood.

Draw a line from the center of the dial to the number 12. Make a mark on this line, half an inch from the center. Place the slanted end of the gnomon on this mark, and the rest of the gnomon's base along the line. Using thin nails, so as not to split the wood, nail the gnomon in place. If you wish, you can glue it in place, but if you are going to use the sundial in a location where it

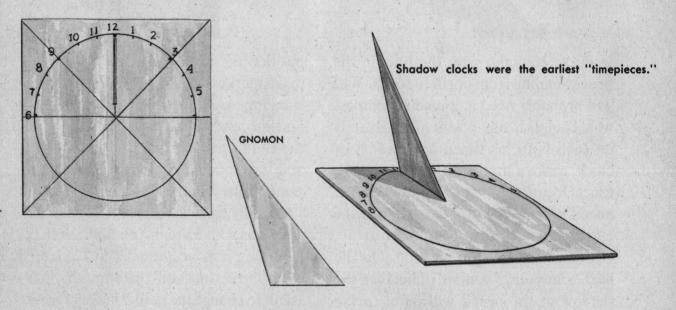

GNOMON

Shadow clocks were the earliest "timepieces."

How you can make a shadow clock.

will be rained upon, it is better to nail down the gnomon. Your sundial is now completed.

Oddly, the best time to set up your sundial is at night. The gnomon must point north. Put the sundial where you want it to remain. Sight along the slant of the gnomon in order to line it up with the North Star. When you have done this, fix the sundial in place, so that it will not easily be moved.

When the sun is shining, you will be able to read the time by noting the number to which the shadow of the gnomon points. But, after all your work, you will be disappointed to find that your sundial is not a very good time-teller. To make your sundial more accurate, you must make an adjustment. On this page is a diagram showing the months and two sets of numbers from 0 to 15. The numbers represent minutes. In the diagram is a curve that is a graph of the *equation of time*. You use the diagram in this manner: Suppose it is February 15. Place a ruler vertically on the dia-gram where you estimate the middle of February to be. Mark the point at which the edge of the ruler crosses the curved line. Now, turn the ruler horizontally, so that its edge touches the point you have just marked on the curved line. Looking to the left you will see that the ruler cuts the left-hand line at a point about fourteen minutes above the middle horizontal line. Now, read the time on your sundial, and add fourteen minutes to your reading. This is the correct time. The rule for the use of the diagram representing the equation of time is this: For readings above the middle horizontal line, add minutes to the sundial reading; for readings below the middle line, subtract minutes from the sundial reading.

Your sundial does not yet agree with your watch. Don't be disappointed; your sundial is correct, and your watch is wrong. Here is why: as the earth turns, each meridian (a line running from the North to the South Pole) is at a different time. For this reason, prior to

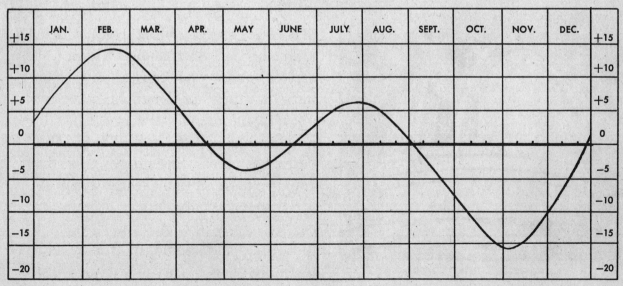

THE EQUATION OF TIME For readings above center line, add minutes to sundial time; for readings below center line, subtract minutes from sundial time.

about one hundred years ago, each town had time different from that of nearby towns to the east and west. The confusion caused by this situation was ended by deciding on standard time zones. All the places within a standard time zone use the same time; that is, all watches and clocks are set to the same time. In the continental United States, there are Eastern, Central, Mountain, and Pacific standard time zones. The time is an hour earlier in each succeeding zone, going from east to west. So, if it is six o'clock in New York, which is in the Eastern Standard Zone, it is three o'clock in San Francisco, which is in the Pacific Standard Zone. The time shown by your sundial is sun time, or solar time, and (adjusted by the equation of time) is the correct time for the place where your sundial is located. If you live where solar time and standard time coincide, your sundial and your watch will both be right.

Our sun is a star, a medium-sized star, and like the billions of other stars in the universe, the sun is a great globe of hot, glowing gas. The

How can you see sunspots?

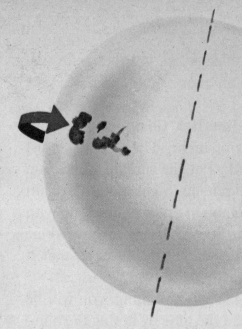

sun is 865,380 miles in diameter, a distance equal to 109 earths in a row. More than 1,000,000 earths would fit into the sun. The temperature at the surface of the sun is 11,000° Fahrenheit, and at the sun's center, the temperature is about 40,000,000° F. The sun is 93,000,000 miles from the earth and the nearly-empty space between has a temperature of 459° F. below zero.

When looking at the sun, we see only its outer surface. This surface is made up of four layers of gas, but we are interested only in the innermost of these layers, the *photosphere*. It is in this layer that sunspots appear. When seen through a large telescope, sunspots look like large, ragged, black holes with a bright border. Astronomers are not at all clear about what causes sunspots or just what they are. Small sunspots are a few thousand miles in diameter, while large ones may be from 50,000 to 150,-000 miles across. Several dozen earths could be tossed into the larger sunspots.

Sunspots usually appear in pairs or clusters. They last for a few days, and then disappear. Some spots may last for more than twenty-five days. Most

PALOMAR OBSERVATORY, CALIFORNIA

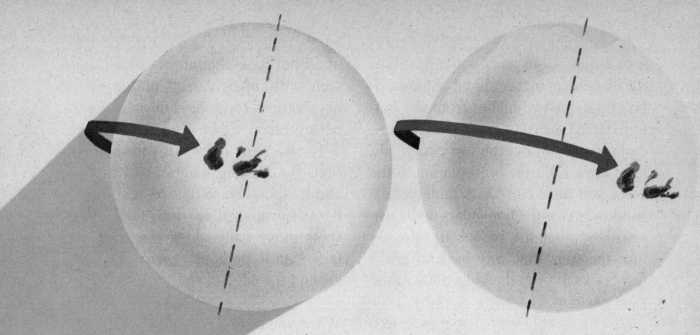

You can prove rotation of the sun by following the location of the same sunspot on successive days.

spots are in the middle regions of both the Northern and Southern hemispheres of the sun.

Of course, the best way to see sunspots is by means of a telescope with the proper ray filters that cut out most of the sun's light. (Do not, however, look at the sun through sunglasses; ordinary sunglasses do not cut out enough light. A pair of field glasses without a darkened sun filter should not be used either. Looking directly at the sun without proper protection may cause injury to the eyes.) Lacking the needed ray filter, we can turn to nature to provide one for us. All we have to do is to make our observations at sunrise or sunset on a clear day, when the sun rises or sets red. A red sun tells us that there is a considerable amount of haze in the earth's atmosphere at that particular time, and the haze cuts out enough sunlight so that we can look directly at the sun without hurting our eyes.

Large sunspots can be seen with the naked eye, and medium-sized ones can be seen with a pair of field glasses. By looking through one or two sheets of red cellophane, or by placing the cello-

EARTH

SUNSPOT

Some sunspots are many times the size of the earth.

phane over the lenses of field glasses, we can lighten the color of the sun and thereby increase the visibility of the dark spots on its surface. If you are watching a rising sun, end your observations when the sun's color becomes orange — as seen by your naked eye, not through the red cellophane. Do not begin to observe the setting sun until it has actually turned red.

There is a way to observe sunspots at any time of day. Stand a pair of binoculars (field glasses) on their front lens casings upon a stout piece of cardboard that is ten inches square. Place the binoculars in the middle of the cardboard, about two inches from the bottom. Run a pencil point around the lens casings, and cut out the two circles you have drawn. Fit the binoculars into the holes you have cut. On a table near a window, place the binoculars and cardboard, so that the binoculars directly face the sun. You may have to use a few books to prop the binoculars in the right position.

Paste a sheet of white paper to a piece of cardboard, in order to stiffen the paper. Focus the binoculars at infinity, or whatever is the focus for seeing farthest. Hold the white paper behind the binoculars, so that the sun's image falls on this white screen. You will probably have to move the screen back and forth — away and toward the binoculars — in order to put the sun in clear focus. When the sun is in focus, you will see sunspots as black dots on the white screen. Don't be discouraged if you do not see any sunspots the first time you

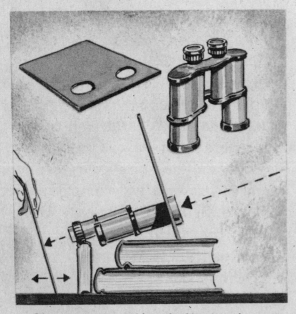

Observe sunspots without looking into the sun.

try. Sometimes the sun's surface is free of all but spots that are too small to be seen with binoculars. Continue your observations for several days, and your perseverance will be rewarded.

Keep a daily record of your observations by drawing diagrams of the sun and its spots. Since the sun revolves on its axis, you will see long-lasting sunspots move daily along the sun's surface, and perhaps even disappear around the edge of the sun.

When you have a good sunspot in focus **How can you measure the size of a sunspot?** on the white screen behind your binoculars, measure carefully the diameter of the image of the sun and of the sunspot. Suppose your image of the sun is two inches in diameter, and the spot is one-sixteenth of an inch. Then, the spot will have a diameter equal to one-thirty second that of the sun. The diameter of the sun is 865,380 miles, and the diameter of the sunspot is one-thirty second of this distance, or 27,043 miles — a fair-sized spot. Sometimes your observations may not give results so easy to calculate as in the foregoing example. Another way to calculate the sunspot's diameter is this: Multiply the sunspot's image by the diameter of the sun (865,380), and divide your result by the diameter of the sun's image on your screen. The result will be the sunspot's diameter.

Perhaps on a clear night you have seen **How can you become a meteor watcher?** a point of light streak across the sky. You may know that what you saw was a

Near Winslow, Arizona there is a crater nearly a mile wide. It was made by a meteor that must have exploded into thousands of pieces.

"shooting star," whose scientific name is *meteor*. The space through which the earth is traveling contains a great amount of small objects — pieces of iron and stone. Most of these range in size from that of a grain of dust to that of a grain of rice. A few are much larger. These objects in space are called *meteoroids*, a word that means "resembling meteors." Most meteoroids travel at high speeds; the average speed is twenty-six miles per second. The earth moves around the sun at a speed of eighteen-and-one-half miles per second. When a meteoroid and the earth meet head on, their combined speeds are forty-four-and-one-half miles per second; when a meteoroid catches up to the earth, its speed of collision is twenty-six minus eighteen-and-one-half, or seven-and-one-half miles per second.

When a meteoroid enters the earth's atmosphere, it becomes a meteor. All except the smallest begin to glow brightly at heights of fifty to seventy-five miles, due to the friction caused by their high speed and the resistance of the atmosphere. By the time meteors have plunged to within forty miles of the earth's surface, most of them have burned up, leaving only a momentarily glowing streak of dust behind. Some of the meteors strike the earth's surface and by doing so become *meteorites* that vary in size from grains of sand (most of them) to the bulk of an automobile. A huge meteorite found by Arctic explorer Robert E. Peary in Greenland in 1897 may be seen at the Hayden Planetarium in New York City. It has a weight of 34½ tons. Meteorites increase the weight of the earth by a thousand tons each day!

On a clear moonless night, in a location where you have an unobstructed view of the sky and no interfering man-made lights, settle yourself in a comfortable rest, such as a deck chair. Within five to ten minutes, your eyes will become adapted to the dark. To observe meteors properly, you must know directions in the sky. Face the North Star—then behind you is south, to your left is west, and to your right is east. Even better, learn the names of some of the constellations, so that you can locate meteors even more closely than by simply using compass directions. Have with you a pad of paper and pencil, a flashlight covered with red cellophane, and a watch and a ruler.

When you see a meteor, record the hour and minute, and, if possible, the exact second of its appearance. Hold

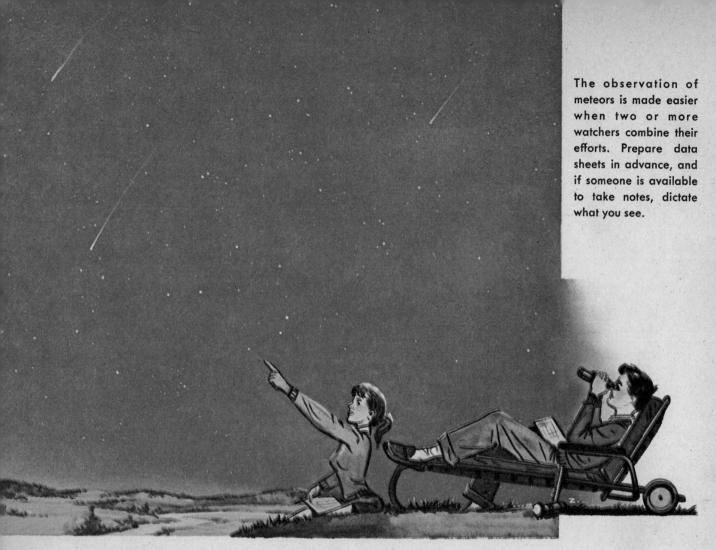

the ruler at arm's length, so that its edge is along the meteor's path. Now, record where the meteor appeared and where it disappeared. Also, record its brightness (very bright, medium, or dim), speed (fast, medium, or slow), how many seconds you think it lasted, and any other comments you wish to make on the meteor's appearance.

If you find this work interesting, you may want to become an official meteor observer. If so, write to the American Meteor Society, 521 North Wynnewood Avenue, Narberth, Pennsylvania. Tell them that you would like to have official report forms and directions for making reports; also, that you would like to obtain sky charts. By reporting to the American Meteor Society, you actually will be participating in the work of astronomers.

On an average night, you may see five to ten meteors an hour. On other nights, when you are experienced enough to spot the faint meteors, you may see forty or fifty. Perhaps you will be as lucky as the observers on the night of November 12, 1833, when 35,000 meteors were observed per hour! Some were as large as the full moon and left trails that lasted fifteen to twenty minutes.

Whether you have performed the experiments in this book or have simply read them, you probably have learned many things about the world around you. And this is always a pleasant experience.